JAZMIN
& the Mystery of the Strawberry Cake

Published in Spring, Texas

Library of Congress Control Number: 2024919986

ISBN:
979-8-9868566-5-0 Hardcover
979-8-9868566-6-7 Paperback
979-8-9868566-8-1 EPUB

Written and Illustrated by Rocío Zanca Oubre

Jazmin was happy. Today, Grandma and Grandpa were coming to visit.

JAZMIN
TOYS

Jazmin ran up and down the steps as fast as she could, leaping all over the house

and even in the yard—she was so excited!

Jazmin knew that every time Grandma and Grandpa visit, they bring gifts and delicious food.

Otto
Jaz

"Otto, Grandma and Grandpa are coming over today," she said. "What's the big deal? I'm taking a nap," grumbled Otto. He covered his ears with his paws.

"Grandma and Grandma are coming to dinner! They're so nice, and they always bring us yummy things to eat. Remember?" Jazmin asked.

Otto did remember the last time Grandma and Grandpa came. They had brought a big cake!

He was so happy, he began to dance with Jazmin. They both sang, "Grandma and Grandpa are coming to dinner, Grandma and Grandpa are coming to play!"

"Grandma and Grandpa are coming," said Dad. We already know that, thought Jazmin and Otto, but then Dad added, "You two must behave yourselves and not get into any trouble."

They ran into the kitchen where Dad and Mom were cooking something.

Yum! That smells delicious, was all Otto could think.

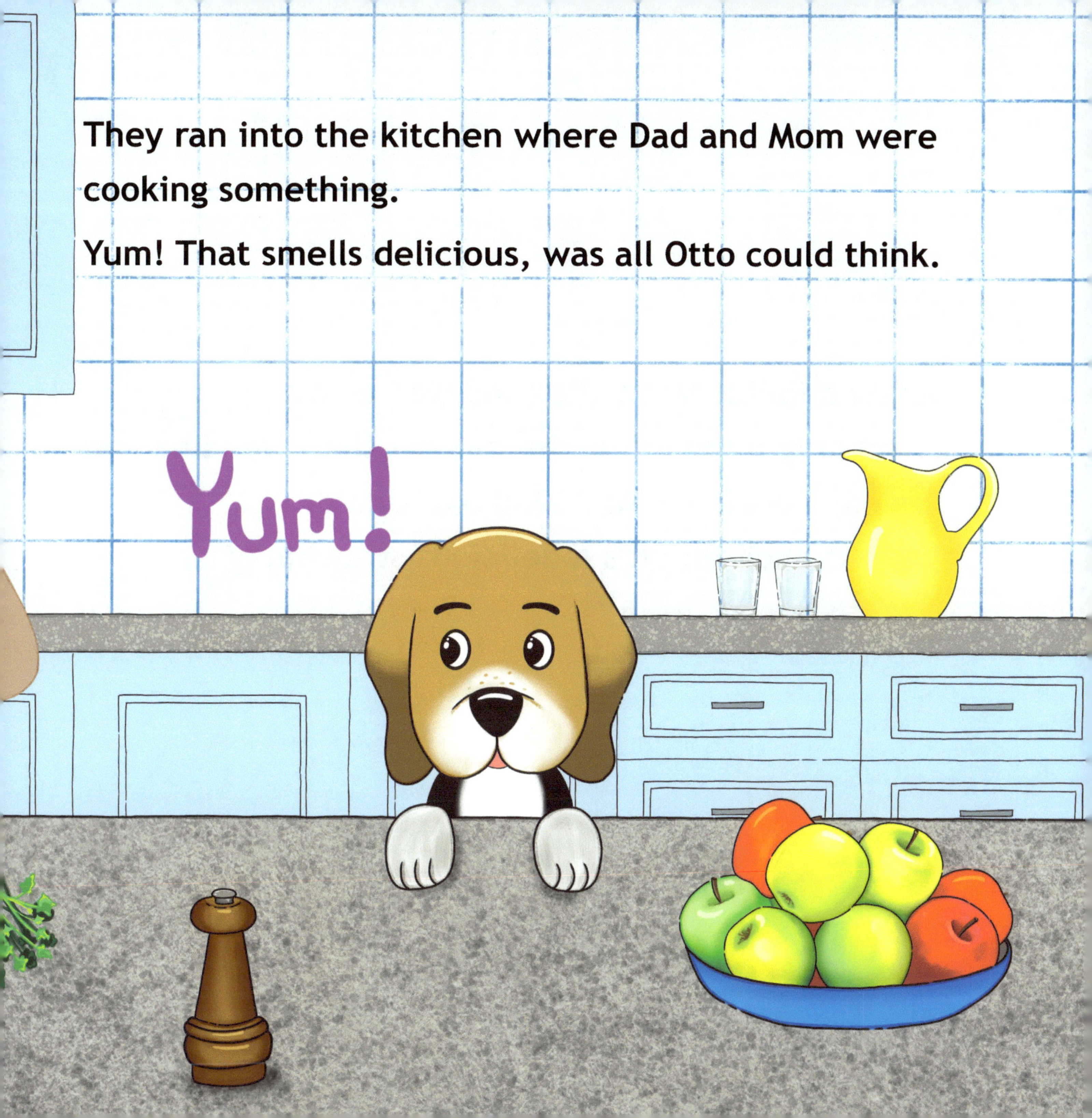

A few minutes later, the food was ready.
"The only thing left is the dessert that Grandma and Grandpa are bringing!" Dad exclaimed.
He was excited. "It's a delicious strawberry cake—my favorite!"

Now Jazmin and Otto had to get ready. Mom brushed Jazmin's fur, tied a pretty ribbon in her hair,

and put a blue tie on Otto. "You're both ready!"
said Mom.

Just then, the doorbell rang: "DING DONG."

"Grandma and Grandpa!" shouted Jazmin and Otto.

They raced to the door, Otto making commotion, as always.

Mom hurried to open the door. Grandma and Grandpa stood there, smiling and full of love. They were carrying many things: a loaf of French bread, cookies to share, and Dad's favorite—strawberry cake.

"Jazmin and Otto, we brought you some gifts," said Grandma and Grandpa.

The pups were happy and ran to open their gifts.

Jazmin was so happy to see Grandma and Grandpa, spend time with them, and play in the park with them before dinner.

Then it was time. Everyone was ready, just waiting for the official announcement.

"Let's eat!" Dad called.

"Wait a minute!" Dad was confused. "Where is the strawberry cake?"

The strawberry cake was not on the table.

It had disappeared! Everyone began to look for it, because Grandma and Grandpa brought it especially for the family dinner.

What had happened? Nobody knew.
The disappearance of the strawberry cake became a
big mystery.

Jazmin looked in the pantry, but it wasn't there.

She searched the laundry room, but she found only dirty clothes.

She inspected the fireplace, but it wasn't there, either.

Then Jazmin looked among the throw pillows on the sofa. The strawberry cake wasn't there, either.

Dad was convinced. "We've looked everywhere, but it's not anywhere!" he said.
Grandpa, who was, of course surprised and upset replied, "We can't enjoy the delicious strawberry cake!"

However, Jazmin would not give up. She kept searching, using her little nose to sniff all over the house. "Ah-ha! Pink cake crumbs, and they go straight to Otto's bed," she thought out loud.

Jazmin was upset. "Otto, it was you! You ate the whole cake," she scolded him.

Otto was still licking his lips. "No! It wasn't me."

"Don't lie, Otto. I can still see the crumbs in your mustache," Jazmin told him.

"What's going on? What's all the commotion?" Dad said, interrupting.

Then he asked, "Otto, do you have something to say?"

Otto hung his head, embarrassed. "I'm sorry. It smelled delicious, and it looked delicious. That's why I decided to eat the whole thing," he admitted.

"Didn't you think about the rest of us? Grandma and Grandpa brought the cake to share with the whole family. It's not fair for you to eat all of it, and it isn't nice to be selfish." Dad was angry. He explained, "Sharing with people we love is one of the most beautiful things in life."

Just then, Mom came in and surprised everyone.
What was she holding? Another strawberry cake!
"I went to the store, and look what I got!" The
strawberry cake she was holding looked exactly like
the first one. Everyone shouted, "Hurray!"

Then Otto apologized to the family for eating the whole cake. He learned that sharing with others is the best way to show them our love.

About the Author

Rocío Zanca Oubre is a children's book author and illustrator who loves creating stories filled with kindness, courage, and heart. She believes that small acts of love can make a big difference — just like Jazmin does. When she's not writing, she enjoys spending time with her family and dreaming up new adventures.

Follow Jazmin on Instagram at:

https://www.instagram.com/jazmin_the_yorkie/

Follow the Author on Instagram at:

https://www.instagram.com/rocio_zanca_oubre_author/

For Free Printable Colouring Pages, visit the website:

www.rociozancaoubre.com

www.ingramcontent.com/pod-product-compliance
Lightning Source LLC
Chambersburg PA
CBHW041605110726
48005CB00002B/296